If You Were
A Cat

NOTE TO PARENTS: IF YOU WERE A . . . is told through
the eyes of the animal as a means of providing children
with facts in an engaging and interactive manner.
With each book, children hone their powers of observation
and gain an understanding of the world around them.

Produced by Daniel Weiss Associates, Inc.
27 West 20 Street, New York, NY 10011.

Published by Silver Press, a division of
Silver Burdett Press, Inc., Simon & Schuster, Inc.
Prentice Hall Bldg., Englewood Cliffs, NJ 07632
For information address: Silver Press.

Library of Congress Cataloging-in-Publication Data

Calder, S.J.
If you were a cat / by S.J. Calder; illustrations by Cornelius Van Wright.
p. cm. — (First facts)
Summary: Describes the characteristic and behavior of cats and
what it would be like to be a cat.
1. Cats—Juvenile literature. [1. Cats.] I. Van Wright,
Cornelius, ill. II. Title. III. Series: First facts.
(Englewood Cliffs, N.J.)
SF445.7.C35 1989   89-6082
636.8 — dc19   CIP
                                                             AC
ISBN 0-671-68604-6   ISBN 0-671-68598-8 (lib. bdg.)

Printed in the United States of America
10 9 8 7 6 5 4 3 2 1

First Facts™

If You Were
A Cat

Written by S. J. Calder
Illustrated by Cornelius Van Wright

Silver Press

Turn around! I'm over here.
I am a cat.
I am playful and curious.
People say I make a very good pet.

My soft fur is orange, black, and white.
My boots are white, too.
Other cats have different colorings and markings.

Some cats have stripes. Some have spots. Some have short fur. Some have long fur.

Angora

Siamese

Abyssinian

Rex

Persian

How many short-haired cats do you see?
How many long-haired cats do you see?

I keep my fur clean by licking it
with my rough tongue.
I can reach almost every part of my body.

But I can't lick my face and ears.
Instead, I lick my front paws to wet them.
Then I *rub, rub, rub*.
What do you do to get clean?

I have whiskers over my eyes,
at the sides of my nose, on my chin,
and on my cheeks.

My whiskers help me in the dark.
If there is something I cannot see well,
my whiskers will feel it.

Close your eyes. Use your hands
to feel what is around you.
You are using your hands
the same way I use my whiskers.

At night I go outside and explore!
I can see much better than you can in the dark.
My eyes open wide to let in more light.

I am quick and quiet on my padded feet.
If I want to climb a tree,
I bring out my claws to help me up.
My tail helps me to keep my balance.

I jump to get down.
You can hardly hear me land.

When I meet other cats,
I meow to greet them.
When I am scared or angry,
I growl or hiss.
And when I am happy, I purr.
What do you do when you are happy?

If my tail is straight up,
it means I am friendly.

If I roll over and wave
my paws in the air,
it means I want to play.

But watch out.
Now my claws are out.
My ears are pulled back,
and my whiskers are forward.
I am ready to fight!

I am a hunter.
I chase and catch birds, squirrels,
and mice.
If I am wearing a bell around my neck,
the animals hear me coming.
They have time to run or fly away.

Even when I am not hunting,
I behave like a hunter.
If you move a toy on a string,
I will chase it.
I run after everything that moves.
I am a playful pet.

Not all cats are pets.
Many cats live in the wild.

Puma/Mountain Lion

Bobcat

Lion

Lioness

Panther

Leopard

Cheetah

Tiger

Can you find the mother, the father, and their babies?

I am a mother cat, too.
When my kittens were born they were tiny
and could not see or hear.
Their eyes and ears were closed.
I licked my kittens to keep them clean.
I fed them milk.
I kept them warm and safe.

Now my kittens are three weeks old.
Their eyes and ears are open.
Their teeth have started to grow.
They play together and run around to explore.
Look at the black kitten!

Where is she going?
I gently pick her up in my mouth
and bring her back.

My kittens are growing every day.
I've stopped feeding them milk.
Now they drink water.
They eat meat, eggs, and fish, as I do.

Soon my kittens are ready
to go to their new homes.
A man takes the tabby kitten.
She looks just like me!

The little girl next door is taking the black kitten.
Which kitten would you choose?

When all my kittens are gone,
I settle down for a catnap.
I sleep on the rug, in the chair,
and by a window in the sun.

When I wake up, I'm ready to go
exploring again.
If you listen closely, you may
hear me.
Meow!

636.8
CAL

Calder, S. J.

If you were a cat.

$11.08

DATE DUE	BORROWER'S NAME	ROOM NO.
	Rick Frutrx	T-4
10-	T REVOR	8-
4/24/96	Jesus Avila	T-5
10-27	JOCS IDA	

636.8
CAL

Calder, S. J.

If you were a cat.